# Ibn Ahmad

# *Pie-*
## perfect Imperfection

Archway Publishing books may be ordered through booksellers or by contacting:

Archway Publishing
1663 Liberty Drive
Bloomington, IN 47403
www.archwaypublishing.com
1-(888)-242-5904

ISBN: 978-1-4808-0846-1 (sc)
ISBN: 978-1-4808-0847-8 (e)
ISBN: 978-1-4808-0894-2 (hc)

Library of Congress Control Number: 2014912827

Printed in the United States of America.

Archway Publishing rev. date: 8/28/2014

Hueyanism – accenting our accumulation

steal not my noble friend
eternal death knows no end

# *Preface*

God has bestowed me with three occasions to share Grace.

Firstly, witnessing Ricky Ponting, the former Australian cricket team captain in full flight.

My childhood neighbor Ricky Chung believed the Australians were unbeatable in cricket. Ponting proved him right twice.

As a member of the winning World Cup squad in 1999, he went on to successfully defend the title captaining the team in 2003 and 2007.

No other team has won the World Cup more than twice and they remain the only team with three successive wins. Ricky's 140 not out in the 2003 finals reverberates game-talk milestone.

Occasion number two, travel grows Grace. My life's travels.

And thirdly, being father.

# Introduction

A man's intentions are known as his Qad'r, his prayers' station.

Effervescence.

Hues.

In us humans, it is singular with a morphological manifestation. Twice as something displeasing the first, and pleasurable, the second.

The effervescence our energy emits contains two parts displeasing with the one part pleasurable.

The displeasing can be measured as two 7s while the second pleasurable one is referred to as a third eight.

The two 7s measure our displeasing content, while an amalgamation measures the earned third 8.

The eight represents togetherness. An amalgamation of the 7s with a reward, pleasure.

The amalgamation the 8 presents is a provision the 7s purification delivers us to.

Our hues. Taste.

This is our value.

Amalgamated to 22 from three parts.

This book's perspective is that when we clean our 7s, we earn a favorable amalgamation called an 8. A connection.

An enjoyment of favor.

Great satisfaction.

A pleasurable enjoyment measured as Hueyanism.

Hueyanistic pleasures are the focus of all relationships.

Be it a bedroom relationship, an employment relation-ship, or a team relationship.

We must release our distasteful energy to find pleasure.

This pleasure is purified in truth when our associations are kept faithful.

Faith overrides to promote strength.

This book proposes our energies' manifestation is a true representation of our thoughts and desires.

Our motivation to seek pleasure.

So we should be conscious of those who are in the way of our actions.

Our energy's effervescence, hues, intrinsically represent the smiling undertone of who we are.

Our grand view invitations to welcome in our private personal environment.

The evidence of our acts containing faith or lack thereof.

When we believe no one is looking, or at least, when we think no one is looking.

Further, when our energies manifest in the displeasing form, we become divided and express ourselves with acts of rebellion.

In this division, the hindrance in expressing our thoughts and our desires cause us to go blind with raging require-ments for instantaneous gratification.

At the expense of faith.

This then becomes a great source of ruin for us.

This book proposes a path, that if followed, hopes to provide an opening for our 7s to find in an amalgamation and be provided with a flourishing.

A third 8.

A pleasurable enjoyment.

Hueyanism – an escargot punt.

Of 22 being necessary to flourish, the numbers represent a pair.

The amalgamation of 7s into the 8 representing man's faith and a woman's arrow.

# The 7s and the 8 are as follows:

1st 7 - Things Incomplete – they promote ignorant behavior.

Complete them.

2nd 7 - Gift Gratitude – If not withheldingly provided, arrogance is interpreted.

Provide no floating dead wood praises.

3rd 8  - Pie - Amalgamate to earn a license.

Represent hues.

# Contents

# 1st 7 - Things Incomplete:

## Complete them

# Chapter 1 - Excellence

Every human being strives for a measure of excellence.

Key to this striving is our ability to identify through a definition, excellence.

The discovery, manifestation, or measurement of it.

Can we prove to ourselves how an acceptable definition of excellence is form? Or what the excellence we are searching for is?

To identify it as something we are in search of, we attempt to place a definition on it. It resides as our hues as 7 and 8, respectively.

1st measurement (an identification):

> Is its attainment derailed by impatience and do we find it difficult and fleeting to hold on to?

1st 7 - You cannot complete what you are unable to identify.

2nd measurement (a unit):

> Do we find ourselves disgusted or aggrieved as a result of acts we do for others, and for which we believe they are short in their show of appreciation?

2nd 7 – You cannot sparingly apply what you cannot measure.

3rd eight (the amalgamation):

> Do we find it difficult to fully comprehend other's communications and the briefness of their expressions?

The 3rd 8 – You cannot amalgamate what you do not comprehend.

If we can conclude to ourselves that any of the above questions answer yes, we are lacking the unity the 3rd 8 provides.

The amalgamation of the positive which results from the negative being cleansed.

Our negative state change fleetingly escapes us and we remain in a state of loss. Finality of our distaste remains lacking.

Our smile reflects our self-value.

As we are unable to find the value we are seeking or setting as our highest attainable level, our true happiness point of hip-attachment remains fleeting.

The energy we are emitting is in displeasing state of distaste. Our perpetual cycle of dissatisfaction contributes in every ounce of effervescence we radiate.

This distaste restricts us from attaining the flourishing true happiness allows. The eight we are in search of.

The rotunda of enjoyment offered to us humans as infinite bliss; apothecated via our belief in Dad. The unknown of survival embedded in us.

We will want to see our prejudices play out on a platform sustaining life on the conditions that we will have existences beyond our ability to conquer, mitigate or otherwise foster.

This fostering is called empathy inherent to us all.

This empathy highlights all we earn in search of shine.

And our Hueyanism punctuates.

Our fragrance, our needs, our desires or our dissatisfaction.

This book recommends that we can come to realize this if we are willing to question our definition of what we identify as excellence.

Some questions resulting from this stage can be:

Did I not deliver properly?
Did I err?
Where did I err?

This approach attempts to elucidate a path of attaining Excellence Standards through empathy recognition.

Recognition of Hueyanism, and then define for ourselves as we all bare loads while holding our breaths for splendor.

The 7s and the 8 apply here as follows:

1st 7 - In realizing we have an element of distaste, we should become conscious that either our excellence standards definitions or in the delivery of our excellence standard definitions, using whatever medium we chose, we faced hindrance. Our impatience hinders us and we experience difficulty.

2nd 7 - Do we believe our efforts to deliver something in earnest excellence are not appreciated as delivery of excellence? If so, we will feel our efforts are under-appreciated and this feeling results in us seeking appreciation in either an inappropriate form, quantity; or from an inappropriate source.

We sometimes miss opportunities to recognize that to be given the opportunity to provide a measure of our own excellence, we are in fact presented with an opportunity to show our own excellence standard definitions.

Hence, we mistakenly look for appreciation when we should be showing appreciation via the gifting of gratitude.

When we have an expectation of appreciation as oppose to recognizing the opportunity for gifting gratitude and so we contribute to our own distaste and impatience.

This results in unhappiness for us and we then reflect the same in our efforts and measure of excellence.

*3rd 8* - Continuing on from above where we questioned ourselves on our own definition and measurement of excellence; we look at the third 8, the amalgamation.

Could it have been, as we were the ones presented with an opportunity to put forward a measure of excellence, it is we who are being measured?

As we are the ones presented with an opportunity to show our own measurement of excellence standard definitions, we should understand the value of accepting the marker's mark? His offered perfection?

Imperative to our understanding and measurement of excellence standards and their definitions is our ability to understand brevity and the quality of it being inherently an excellent standard by itself?

Understanding this metamorphosis allows for our interpretation of excellence to find finality and flourish into an amalgamation.

Key to this metamorphosis and flourish is our interpretation. we are responsible for amalgamating the 3rd 8. For finding finality to the bitter 7s.

Understanding this as a mark we provide teaches us the recognition our decisions influence our flourishings and faith. Our happiness and our distaste.

Understanding this is an amalgamation of imperfections allows us to find the true happy state this book refers to as pie.

Once our measurement and definition of excellence is viewed favorably, our interpretation of imperfection can be viewed as our excellence standard definition.

Perfection in our eyes.

# Chapter 2 - Solitude

At times, we find ourselves in states of impatience, intolerance and distaste.

We propose it is as a result of our energy manifesting in a distasteful state. Our effervescence or the energy we are emitting into the world has a bitter reception wherever it is received.

We further propose that the laws of nature, man's guide in matters of destiny, or what we refer to as luck, dictates that if we emit a bitter energy, we will in turn be served with a returning bitter energy.

Thus, we recommend that man should conduct a self-assessment using the 7s we propose to guide himself to a state of finality ending his negative view.

That recommendation now leads us to this chapter. Solitude.

The very essence of this book is for man to reflect and locate the distaste that hinders him in life and commit to a path of cleanse.

This cannot be done without solitude. We must take parts of this cleaning journey singularly. To recognize that some measure, large or small, of what we contribute to the world around us, represents our individual energy.

Hence, in reflecting on the make-up of our energy, solitude is imperative.

In resorting to solitude to examine our energy in the hope of locating what makes us impatient, ungrateful and unapologetically judgmental, we must look at our connectivity to the world around us.

The contribution we make and the expectations we place on the environment we subsist on.

In English Law, there are two known concepts as, as follows:

A Right; and
A Privilege.

The right is exemplified where a farmer retains the exclusive rights for the use of a specific track of land.

Where as a privilege is embodied in the action of the farmer wherein he allows another person to temporarily access somewhere otherwise inaccessible without passage over the land to which he, the farmer retains exclusive rights.

He grants a privilege to someone else. He tolerates.

To self-examine our distaste under the banner of solitude, the above two concepts are helpful if we choose to examine the following questions:

1 -    Will becoming the sum of all I am provide a more fulfilling life for me? (examined under solitude)

2 -    Can I become the sum of all I am without making allowances for the ones who tolerated privileges along the way? (examined under Association)

3 -    For whose benefit do I seek to answer these questions? (examined under Virtue and Morality)

We will examine question one in this chapter under the chapter heading, Solitude, and the remaining two questions in the following two chapters, Association; and Virtue and Morality.

The aim of the first 7 chapters in this book is to look at the first 7 making up the 7s; things incomplete.

The goal here is to conquer impatience by completing the incomplete things as they hinder our efforts when left incomplete.

The purification path we propose here is that impatience is conquered through reflections.

Will becoming the sum of all I am provide a more fulfilling life for me?

Lets start by examining the question. What is the sum of all I am? And what is a fulfilling life?

In this book, we propose the sum of all we are can be measured in four amalgamations.

1 -    Our Education
2 -    Our Life Experiences
3 -    Our understanding of Cultural Brevity
4 -    Our fostering of Unification ability.

Our education should be viewed as a value, which follows from us finding a line of symmetry and not necessarily a right for us to ascend.

By ascend we mean the automatic assumption of hierarchical status above another.

It is a valuation line allowing an association among like-minded individuals where the basis of an acceptable good measure is already determined.

Our experience on the other hand can be more duplicitous.

Duplicitous because it incorporates our associations and experiences from professional and educational endeavors as well as private family associated endeavors; which are usually influenced by taste and choice.

Hence, we allow ourselves both, a right and a privilege. The right in formal and professional endeavors and the privilege in personal, private associations.

Our understanding of Cultural Brevity refers to our ability to bond with our own cultural heritage through briefness and subtlety.

How easily we find it embraceable.

The way we view it and the way we perceive others viewing it.

The smell of our foods, the dress of our people, the pitch of our speech.

It is common to find that the things we believe we should shield or hide in our expressions with others are in fact the oldest ancestral traditions common to our roots.

They are universal to the way of life of people everywhere.

They exist wherever people live.

They are intrinsic in our expressions.

As a result of these being part of the core of our culture's existence, we will be presented with two paths.

The first and stronger one is the path of expression we choose when expressing with others of our own culture.

As we are of the same traditions and heritage, we will have a subtle understanding of other's expressions where certain confirmations will be taken for granted.

Hence the phrase, understanding Cultural Brevity.

For example ordering food similar to that which we prepare at home, at a restaurant of our own culture.

We will have a form of abbreviation, whether overtly or covertly, evidenced through trust.

This will become evident as a result of us being familiar with the contents of the dish and the mode of preparation we in our culture find acceptable. Like how mom or grandma use to do it.

It is the root call of our comfort level.

We will take for granted the restaurant preparing the dish is familiar with the taste of the people they are serving relevant to the category of the establishment they hold themselves out to be.

That is, a Thai and an Indian restaurant being familiar with Thai and Indian dishes for the Thai and Indian population in the neighborhood they are serving.

The second path of offer to us is the path we take when expressing with others from outside our culture. Non-culture members.

Continuing with the example of the restaurant, but with the restaurant serving Thai or Indian dishes to non-Thais or non-Indians.

The dish will need to be explained to the non-culture member.

The true test of embracing our own cultural is here.

Will we have the confidence, as the preparer of the dish serving a non-culture member, to simply introduce the dish as an identity item of our culture and let the non-culture member make his own conclusion?

Or will we find it necessary to elaborate on how the non-culture member should interpret the dish?

Elaboration in this case can take away from our confidence in our own culture in the form of saying too little or too much. It may reflect over compensation.

This over compensation may reflect us having an inferior view of our own culture's images, likes and dislikes when we are interacting with others of a different culture.

Hence, understanding Cultural Brevity is the phrase chosen as one of the four lines of amalgamation to consider in answering the question, will becoming the sum of all I am provide a better life for me?

If we are able to embrace the customs, beliefs and mannerisms of our own culture first, and then the beliefs and mannerisms of people of other cultures, it will indicate we recognize there is a universal system of beliefs and mannerism inherent to people of all cultures.

This then will reflect not our knowledge of other culture's beliefs and mannerism but our own acceptance and self-value.

We embrace our first. Always. None is immune to this. It is inherent. Inescapable if completion if what you seek.

The strength and value of this acceptance, manifests itself in the brevity of our expressions.

We know we belong and where.

This belonging provides us with a unification opportunity.

Our single identity which manifests from the unified amalgamations. The amalgamation of our education, our experiences, and where we sit. Where we belong.

It must be among our own people first and foremost.

So, Will becoming the sum of all I .am provide a better life for me?

The answer lies in our amalgamation. Can we amalgamate a 3rd 8 here?

If the amalgamation of our education, experience, cultural brevity and unification leads us to believe the sum of all we are amalgamates a 101 while the cost of sustaining us amalgamates 99, we should conclude we have a positive (101-99=2) contribution towards excellence standard definitions and can undertake endeavors of our own choosing.

We are unity as a single entity and can say the sum of all we are is greater than the cost of up keeping us.

We are who we represent ourselves to be and can provide valued contribution.

This conclusion allows us a Right, to become the sum of all we are.

# Chapter 3 - Association

Can I become the sum of all I am without making allowances for the ones who tolerated privileges along the way?

Continuing on from chapter 2 - Solitude, where we concluded that if, on unification, our self-value amalgamation is a Right, we are validated in saying the sum of all I am will provide a better life for me.

Our next step then is to answer the question;

Can I become the sum of all I am without making allowances for the ones who tolerated enjoinments along the way?

The short answer is no.

This should cause us to review our associations.

More precisely, can we hold on to the Right (101) we earned under Solitude? The answer to this lies in realizing an amalgamated Right. A 3rd 8.

To do this, we will need to take at look at our associations.

In keeping with the Right and Privilege standard set early, we can say a Right is where we provide an effort value 101 and received a compensation of 99.

For example, changing a friend's flat tire while she offers you a ride. It would be a 101 if the friend were dressed in fancy attire.

Our rationale for this conclusion is this.

Regardless of her ability to do it herself, she would have conclude the assistance was greater than the cost of the ride when placed against the potential cost of having to do it herself accounting for her fancy dress and all.

In this case the cost is her giving the ride.

Either way, she was traveling in a car with available passenger seating so we can conclude she possessed the availability at the time of making the offer.

The cost of providing the ride must be ascertained based on the opportunity cost of the ride, at the time of offering the ride. Not after and in the light of the assistance to fix the flat.

The offer was made based on her having available passenger seating in the car.

Hence, the cost of giving the ride at the time of offering cannot outweigh the assistance received in changing the flat.

So in the end, she benefited from having the passenger in the car with her.

On the other hand, the association may qualify as a Privilege if the ride received is from a female driver dressed in gym attire and shared associations with rally drivers or were part of a pit crew. Here, we are proving she is fit and capable of changing the tire herself.

One should be able to objectively conclude here, that receiving the ride was a privilege granted and that with or without you as a passenger, she was capable of changing the tire herself.

Regardless of the labor to change the wheel, receiving the ride was more beneficial to you who received it.

You received a privilege.

The Right goes to the driver for offering the ride. You compensated with 99 while she gifted you 101.

This is the essence of this chapter. Its attempts to elucidate basic principles associations are formed on.

If we choose to become the sum of all we can be, we must make allowances for the Privileges extended to us by others.

It is imperative if we are to bring closure to things incomplete and conquer our impatience. The first step to increasing our chances of amalgamating our 7s into the 3rd 8.

In applying the above scenario of 101 (a Right) and 99 (a Privilege), we need to consider if in summating the associations we enjoyed, we amalgamate a 101 or 99.

If the summation concludes we amalgamate a 99, we were at times offered Privileges in our associations beyond the value of our contributions and we should conclude we cannot become the sum of all we are without making accommodations for those who extended Privileges to us along the way.

We cannot, as we are indebted to them who forged Privileges for us to benefit.

Irrespective of the presence of a claim to the debt, the 7s cannot fully materialize an amalgamated 3rd 8.

We will fall short of the amalgamation necessary to deliver us from our distasteful state. We must first repay acceptably.

Only on this premise can we move forward to posit excellence standards definition on the environment on which we subsist.

Or the base on which we develop our excellence standard definitions will fall-out if those who offered us Privileges choose to collect their debts.

We will further elaborate on this in section 2 of the book, Gifting Gratitude.

If we conclude we balance a 101, it indicates we can proceed on a path to become the sum of all we are.

A balance of 101 means we are willing to forge for others if necessary and extend to them Privileges.

This can be interpreted as a solidifying one of our earlier conclusions. We are willing and able to provide efforts and endeavors valued at 101 in return for compensations 99.

Therefore, we are valid in saying *becoming* the sum of all I am will provide a better life for me.

# Chapter 4 - Virtue and Morality

For whose benefit do I seek to answer these questions?

Continuing on in this first section of the book, or the first 7, things incomplete, completing them to conquer our impatience, it should become evident by now that we are focusing on ourselves, a self-valuation.

As we found a deficiency manifested through distaste, we embarked on a path to define what we consider excellence for ourselves.

We concluded that under things incomplete, conquering impatience is key to winning the battle of the first 7.

In the opening chapter, Excellence, we concluded we must find our own definition and measurement to find satisfaction. And that if we are unable to do so, distaste will continue.

It will continue as we are unable to define adequately what we consider excellence, our measurement of it and its receipt by our intended audience when we posit.

Our deficiency in a definition of excellence lead us to a path of self-evaluation. That took us to solitude where we examined Rights, Privileges and the sum of all we are.

Our chapter on solitude then led us to review our associations.

In that chapter we concluded we must determine whether we have a conclusive right to become the sum of all we are.

This was done by reviewing our associations where we concluded we must place value on the allowances extended to us along the way by others.

This was done by concluding an answer to the question; can I become the sum of all I am without making allowances for the ones who tolerated an enjoinment along the way?

We concluded we could continue on our purification path to become the sum of all we are and define our own excellence standard definitions if a Right is earned (101).

We will now continue with the aim of retaining the Right earned under solitude, (concluding the sum of all we are equals 101), and the Right earned under association (my associations forged for me so I will forge for others) and attempt to accumulate a third Right. The rationale here is that each Right will amalgamate towards our 3rd 8.

Amalgamating a 3rd 8 will serve the purpose of saying we have a right to choose excellence standard definitions of our own comfort.

That now brings us to this chapter, Virtue and Morality.

If we choose to examine the virtue and morals we recognize, we must answer the following question:

For whose benefit do I seek to answer these questions?

The chapters on Solitude and Association can contribute to us finding a consensus on our choice of virtues and morals. The following sources should be considered as starting points.

Our education; our life experiences and our cultural synchronicity.

The virtue and morals we stand in defense of should be based on our education, our life experiences and our cultural heritage.

The virtues and morals we accept to recognize and defend must reflect us as personal contributors.

If you can walk it, include it. If you cannot, do not include it in your excellence standard definitions.

A second source from which our virtues and morals can come is our associations.

As we pointed out, we enjoy associations of both Rights and Privileges.

The associations where Rights (101) were extended and privileges were received must be revered with inclusion. They were willing to forged for us when were short (99) and now that we genuinely want to be the sum of all we are, recognition must be tolerated.

Recognition in this regard will be to include in the virtues and morals we recognize, virtues and morals they (our associations) recognized.

The virtues and morals that allowed them tolerance to include us in their associations when we were lacking Rights to enjoy pleasures they rightfully possess.

Hence, our virtues and morals should come from two sources and they should provide an answer to the question, for whose benefit do I seek to answer the three questions.

They come from our education, life experiences and cultural synchronicity ability as we develop as into an individual; and those who tolerated enjoyments for us along the way.

This path of recognition offers us the opportunity to amalgamate our 3$^{rd}$ 8 from the previous two Rights earned under Solitude and Associations.

When these Rights (101) amalgamate into our 3rd 8, we begin to understand how excellence standards are defined and our chances of defining attainable excellence standards are enhanced.

This then becomes a contributor to our impatience being conquered. We understand the necessity of completion. Of things left incomplete.

# Chapter 5 - Knowledge

Upon completion of our understanding of the innate structure necessary to define excellence, a realization should now start to step in.

Knowledge is an accumulation and it sets par.

Par refers to how we find excellence in others as well as our self. Congruency.

Of vital importance here is this.

Your present knowledge accumulated through this book's self-examination process over the chapters lead to here.

This process had to be set out and detailed by the book's author to elucidate in you, the reader, the accumulation.

An elucidation.

As a result, the path to get here must be valued equally as the new found ability to set excellence standard definitions.

Hence, we are now at this chapter, Knowledge. It must be credited as an accumulation.

An accumulation, that takes time and accumulating.

As such, its practical applications must be to enhance value. Either for the owner of the knowledge, the audience targeted, or both.

The excellence standard definitions proposed after knowledge is accumulated must reflect the Right over the Privilege concept.

A Right is a gift to those of lesser possessions whilst a Privilege is an imposition. Ones Excellence Standard Definitions must accommodate this position.

This will take us to the next two chapters on things in-complete – completing them to conquer impatience, Justice; and Equilibrium and Beauty.

# Chapter 6 - Justice

Among the many definitions offered for the word Justice by the Merriam-Webster online dictionary, the following one is offered:

> the maintenance or administration of what is just especially by the impartial adjustment of conflicting claims or the assignment of merited rewards or punishments.

This definition takes the position justice is an administration occurring after a conflict arises or when adjustments becomes necessary. Awarding a reward through the punishing of one for acts causing harm to another.

The essence of this view is justice becomes relevant after one suffers.

He then applies to the courses of remedy available to him for intervention and rectification favoring him.

As this book aims to elucidate a path of adherence for man to adopt if he wishes to increase his chances of finding true happiness through self- purification, we propose man apply the concept of justice in a predicative form.

As we pointed out, the above definition justifies an appeal for justice only after a conflict has arisen.

This book proposes a path that is more beneficial if man wishes to adhere to just concepts in his endeavors, with the aim of avoiding conflicts.

As was pointed out earlier, man embarks on a path to locate what he considers excellence standard and their definitions as a result of him suffering from one of the 7s, impatience.

For success on that path, we elucidate finding self-value.

Self-value was found through finding ourselves through solitude, association and knowledge.

We then concluded man can exercise a right to become the sum of all he is when he is willing to make allowances for those who tolerated enjoinments along the way

Essentially, he has earned an amalgamated right (101). The 3rd 8 necessary to understand and define excellence standards to enjoy pure pleasure.

We now propose, that, for his excellence standards defining endeavors to be received and enjoyed as such, he must serve the excellence he wishes to create by adhering to justice on a predicative basis.

Ibn Ahmad

No injustice in his intentions or actions will reward him
with an enjoyment of just returns at all times.

# Chapter 7 - Equilibrium and Beauty

The art of aesthetic practices beautification through adornment. Appreciation

To earn our first 7, completing things incomplete and conquering impatience, we embarked on a path of understanding excellence standard definitions.

We journeyed through Solitude, Association and Virtue and morals.

With each one contributing to our first 7, and towards an amalgamated 3rd 8, we earned a 7 for conquering impatience at Virtue and Morality by recognizing the pieces necessary to define excellence standard definitions.

Knowledge and Justice then tested this earned 7. The necessity of this testing is this.

The chapters on Solitude, Association, and Virtue and Morality allowed us to define as excellence, our highest amalgamated value, perceptually.

A self-value amalgamated though totaling our education, experience and cultural unity. Saying, the total of all we are must be present in endeavors we partake in.

This is the level of excellence standard definition must be ready to accept questioning.

This questioning came in the chapters on Knowledge and Justice.

The chapter on Knowledge guided us to realize that Knowledge sets par as it accumulates.

As our body of knowledge accumulated over a period of time; of pertinence is our recognition that not everyone will have a similar accumulation at the same time.

Therefore the concept of par must find resonance.

Par represents this. If our accumulated body of knowledge allows us to produce an original can of milk at $100, which can be mass reproduced at $5 after the original one, should we seek to sell 10 cans of milk at $100 or should we seek to sell 100 cans of milk at $10?

As a result of us identifying not everyone will have an identical body of accumulated knowledge at the same time, and the resulting effect will be an unshared valuation of excellence standard definitions, to set the par at a can for a $100 will result in an excellent standard not capable of universal acceptability.

Hence, the excellence standard defined will not find universal acceptance. The motivation for us to define excellence standards in the first place.

On the other hand, setting the par at 100 cans for $10 each represents the inclusion of a justice element on a predicative platform.

To set par at 100 cans at $10 each represents adherence to our earlier declared conclusion, no injustice in my intent or act will reward me an enjoyment of justice at all times.

Our cans of milk are now universally accessible, which was our chief motivator for defining excellence standards.

The relevance of these tests, Knowledge and Justice, to our first earned 7 elucidates an innate quality to the ill of impatience.

Your definition of what conquers impatience lacks patience if tests of par and universality cannot pass persistence.

If the par that is set is not mutually beneficial and widespread acceptance cannot be had, the universality of the excellence standard defined is flawed.

The passing of these tests to retain our earned 7 for conquering impatience, now brings us here, Equilibrium and Beauty, and the following phrase:

The art of aesthetics teaches beautification through adornment.

Any excellence standard we propose in endeavors on the environment on which we subsist must firstly be adorned with equilibrium and beauty to form par.

Especially when they are firstly displeasing.

Only then will the state of distaste hindering us from our truest happy state be conquerable for to complete things incomplete.

2nd 7 - Gift Gratitude:

*Provide no floating dead wood praises*

# Chapter 8 - Fear

In this second section of the book, - Gift Gratitude: provide no floating dead wood praises, our aim is to test our Excellence Standard Definition against potential challenges.

Challenges in the form of what keeps us in a perpetual cycle of impatience and incompleteness.

Hence, we entitle the section gift gratitude.

Our recommendation to defeat a perpetual cycle of impatience is to gift gratitude.

Floating dead wood praises representing flaws we attempt to cover by giving hollow praises. Flaws that may be subject to challenges.

Holes in our theory on excellence standard definitions, and ultimately the derived self-value.

The challenges we will look at in this section continues on from the previous section where we earned a 7 for defining excellence standards.

Our mode of operation here is to double our earned 7 from section one, impatience; and move forward with two earned 7s.

We will then attempt to work past the challenges and retain both 7s.

The gift of this section is we are starting with an earned 7, and doubling it.

As we now have two earned 7s, this section aims to elucidate gratitude gifted as a path to retaining anything of value.

The first challenge this chapter addresses is fear.

The fear of losing the first earned 7.

The following six chapters in this section:

Wrath;
Unity;
Sincerity;
Repentance;
Love;
And Eagerness,

follows the process of define and test to retain used in the first section.

Wrath as a second challenge with Unity as a state of acceptance, Sincerity as a test, Repentance as a remedy, Love as gift and Eagerness as a challenge with a gift of offer.

Referring to gratitude as a gift to be gifted is a first release which defeats the ill of impatience, twice.

This is accomplished as it is gratitude expressed.

Similar to releasing a tugging rope when our hands begin to burn, we are letting go of what, if held on to longer, will be an unnatural human reaction.

Gratitude expressed reflects the kindness inherent to humankind. Withheld, it is of little use except to be encircled by distaste.

The validation associated with the act of firstly gifting defeats the challenge of fear.

As we concluded in the first section, excellence standards definition amalgamates after a self-value examination process.

This should teach us acceptance through adornment.

Essentially, we are gifting gratitude as a defense mechanism to protect what we value and adore.

In defending a valuable possession, one must contemplate its lost. Hence, we start the section with the gift of a double earned 7.

Strength in defense is automatically letting go of the fear of losing. Letting go of value and the setting of par.

While our excellence standard definition was amalgamated after a process of self-examination, we must recognize others view their excellence standard definitions in earnest as well.

Gifting gratitude allows us to escape the fear of losing through an enhanced understanding of value. The value of appreciation given first is recognition of par. We all share a desire for valuables.

In this case, the retention of our doubled earned 7s.

Elucidating this path allows us to defeat the fear of losing, with appreciation.

Appreciation gifted allows us to recognize par. All things of value is formed out of someone's desire for excellence standard definitions.

And as a result, we all inherently possess fear.

# Chapter 9 - Wrath

Wrath as a challenge manifests as blind anger.

Anger that is so blinding, our ability to reason and respond is deprived and we are promoted in favor of decidedly swift instinctive responsive action.

The potency of this form responsive action is the detrimental blindness. The fact that it is responsive must be balanced against the motivation for the act initiating a response from us.

Why are we prompt to respond in anger?

The relevance of this is we are in a position to defend a value we have earned, the 7s.

We must recognize we are responding to an initiated act where the greatest potential loss is to us.

The loss of what we value most, our earned 7s.

We are in possession of value beyond compare. Of personal adornment.

An earned 7 promises to take us to a finality. A finality of the displeasing state hindering us from amalgamating our 3rd 8.

Human instinctive behavior when faced with the potential of losing an item of value favors an energized defense.

Energized in the sense of a defense matching the form of action triggering us, but at a responsive degree higher.

Conquering this instinctive defense is essential.

Possession of the object of value, the doubled earned 7, places the onus of its protection on us.

Doubly from ourselves if our instinctive act of defense is to follow the pattern of the initiated triggering action. Doing exactly what the other guy did, with added zest.

This energized anger needs a controlling mechanism.

We need to create a defense against ourselves so that we do not energize the aggressive trigger action targeted at us.

As we are the ones in possession of a valuable value keeping, our defense for retaining it must mitigated our flaws and trigger impulses.

The conclusion here to defeat wrath as a challenge is to mitigate our own anger.

Thereby, allowing no avenue for a self-loss of our valued possession, the earned 7s.

# Chapter 10 - Unity

On journeying through the 7s to the 3rd 8, and making it to this chapter, Unity, getting past fear and wrath provides a point for atonement. An appreciation.

A gift.

Unity positioned here aims to allow an appreciation as a gift to ourselves.

In recognizing fear as a challenge we possess, we defeat it by gifting ourselves an understanding of the value we fear losing.

The value of the two earned 7s elucidates a focus on the valued possession, the 7s. What we have to defend is of value, not what we are defending against.

Equally, in defeating wrath, we again elucidated the focus of the valuable we are in possession of. If we are forced to defend it, we do not energize the act of aggression targeted at us.

This defensive strategy to mitigate forces challenging our earned 7s and our excellence standard definition should now deliver us to a point of unity.

A unity point in recognizing the possession of an atonement, a valued state, in this instance, an amalgamated excellence standard definition.

We are in possession of the item and we have to defend its value.

And, this value is best defended through a recognition of its value at all times. In the face of all challenges. So that par can be set.

So, our point of unity here is earned through a single defensive strategy, the valuable is our possession, par must be defended.

Unity here is confidence in defending the valued possession through the elevation of its value in the face of all challenges. Not that it is more valuable than all else without regard, but simply from view point it is our possession.

As a unifying source is it represents a right exercised after a thorough examination of our self value.

# Chapter 11 - Sincerity

At this point, we are well on our way to retain our two earned 7s.

We are at ease with our first 7 earned through excellence standard definition and so far, our second gifted earned 7 is holding up against potential challenges.

In the last chapter, Unity, our confidence in our excellence standard definition should have been given a boost.

The next four chapters in this section, including this one aims to be prescriptive if we find our confidence shaky.

As we evolved through the chapters of this book, from chapter 1, Excellence, to the last chapter, Unity, on the strength of our propose excellence standard definition, our understanding of the elucidation this book aims to provide should be evolutionary.

Our understanding of the 7s and our distasteful state in life should have taken us to deep levels of honesty.

Areas of gray in earlier chapters as a result of elucidation from our self-examination following the chapter's prescriptions should have become less and less.

Our level of honesty should be more accurate now.

At this point if we find unity lacking and we are unsure of the confidence we illuminate in our excellence standard definition, the prescription here is to examine the sincerity we applied in the self-evaluation process to here.

Perhaps in applying this book's path to elucidation and conquering the 7s, our honesty and sincerity is lacking one hundred percent commitment.

Any areas of gray in our confidence in the excellence standard definition we wish to posit becoming known here, is becoming known as a result of less than one hundred percent sincerity.

Sincerity here relates to the first section of the book, things incomplete, conquering impatience.

It would be valuable to reiterate here, that the only 7 we have earned to here is for the first section, conquering impatience. The second was gifted.

In the first section, the first chapter, Excellence, elucidated that impatience arises as a result of us having difficulty in excellence standard definitions.

The remaining six chapters of that section elucidated a path to assist with excellence standards definition.

At that point, we elucidated that if after working through the section you can conclude you have a right (101) to undertake endeavors wherein you postulate on the environment in which you subsist your excellence standard definitions, you can do so.

And it should be adorn it with equilibrium and beauty.

You were then offered an earned 7 for conquering impatience, the first to be earned as per the postulations of this book.

The elucidating of a path to clean our distaste, which hinders our ability to find true happiness. Our true happy state.

In the beginning of the second section, gifting gratitude, we begun by gifting the second earned 7 as an advance.

In doing so, we immediately began the practice of gifting and showing gratitude. We have elucidated so far in this section, that the best defense in defending a value we possess is to always recognize its value.

This recognition allows us to set par as par allows justification.

This solidifies our position as the owner of the valued possession and that the responses we provide to mitigate the challenges we encounter are of our own.

As gratitude gifted is the greatest form of expressed gratitude, the retention of our valued possession is ensured.

Hence, we now test the confidence of our unity.

If our state of unity possesses shades of gray, the sincerity we applied in our cleansing to this point needs review.

This review will illuminate the remedial work necessary, via the following three chapters:

Repentance;
Love;
And Eagerness.

# Chapter 12 - Repentance

Repentance is a gift on offer.

It means we continuing in the spirit of this section gifting gratitude, and as such, it is offered as a gift, to aid the retention of the second earned 7.

The preceding chapter alluded that the presence of gray areas in our unity results if, in a review of the sincerity we applied to this point in the book, our unity is shaky.

A deficiency in the sincerity we applied to define excellence standard definitions can be found in either of the following.

Insincerity in our excellence standard definition itself, or insincerity in our conclusion to posit excellence standard definitions.

Insincerity in our excellence standard definition should become evident if we find it difficult to defend when they are met with challenges.

Evidence of this insincerity would lie in the summation of the self-value par set from the four measures amalgamation:

Our Education
Our Life Experiences
Our understanding of Cultural Brevity
Our fostering of Unification ability.

The excellence standard we wish to posit would be difficult to defend if the amalgamation was incorrect and our totaling reflected a right (101) when it should have reflected a privilege (99).

An error in the totaling of our evaluation from the four measures will necessitate a review of the right (101) we awarded ourselves.

Recapping here, the right (101) over the privilege (99) allowed us to conclude we have a right to become the sum of all we are and reflect this in our excellence standard definition.

This right was then exercised in us concluding we will posit excellence standard definitions representing the sum of all we are on the environment on which we subsist.

Should the review conclude our amalgamation should have awarded us a privilege (99) as opposed to right (101), the second avenue for insincerity as outlined above, we cannot posit our excellence standards definition on the environment on which we subsist.

If we have already done so, we need to engage in repentance to make amendments.

Amendments in this instance will take the form of us refraining from further espousal and making sincere attempts to identity potential harm resulting from usage of the excellence standards definitions posited.

This should be viewed as an added opportunity to test our sincerity.

An added opportunity to test our ability via undertaking the task to identifying potential harm resulting from our espousal and the taking of corrective action to compensate for the unlawful espousal.

We possessed no right (101) to posit them on the environment in which we subsist.

We are indebted to others for the privileges they extended to us.

Their rights are greater.

As we learnt, we can only posit excellence standard definition if when accounting for allowances enjoyed along the way from those who tolerated us, we amalgamate a right (101).

Repentance here should allow us to enjoin ourselves with a renewed level of sincerity.

At this point, we should repeat the first section eluci-dated path of self-evaluation and retry earning the first 7, completing things incomplete to conquer impatience, if so desired, or continue to the next two chapters and then consider a re-evaluation.

# Chapter 13 - Love

Among the definitions provided for *love* in the Merriam-Webster dictionary, is the following one:

the object of attachment, devotion, or admiration.

The positioning of love here at chapter 13 earns its place as a nixing opportunity to repair.

The chapter on sincerity examined whether our self-evaluation in section one to amalgamate an excellence standard definition was flawed.

Whether our exercised right to posit the definition was lawful.

The following chapter on repentance alluded that if the posited excellence standard definition was unlawfully posited, we should undertake a path of repentance in the form of immediately withdrawing the excellence standard definition and take steps to amend for any losses our position may have caused.

We then alluded all was not lost and with the newly found level of sincerity we can repeat the first section elucidated path of self-evaluation and re-attempt earning the first 7.

That recommendation now leads us to this chapter as a repair.

If on the conclusion of the last chapter, we need to reexamine our excellence standard definition, we have a choice.

Firstly, we can attempt a re-evaluation of our self-value to potentially earn the earned 7 in review.

This chapter attempts to provide the context for the re-evaluation.

The above definition of love alludes the following characteristics are present.

In the undertaking of a process of self value evaluation or excellence standard definition, a path of purification must be followed, as was done in the first section of this book.

This path must determine whether that which we enjoin or wish to enjoin ourselves with is a right (101) or a privilege (99).

Hence, our adherence to the purification path in section one provided a path for attachment.

One had to make a decision to tolerate guidance by it. Even reading the book to this point requirement a commitment. An attachment.

The remedy offered here under the heading of love is as follows.

We can retake the evaluation and attempt to earn a right (101) and the earned 7, or we can recognize that the process, regardless of the outcome, whether a right (101) or privilege (99), requires the involvement of love to complete.

This recognition should guide us to appreciate the excellence standard definition endeavor and its inherent requirements, and offers us a choice.

Retake the evaluation process in an attempt to earn a right (101) and subsequently an earned 7, or, in recognizing the inherent requirement of love to be present in the form of devotion to the endeavor, we accept the amalgamation of a privilege (99) and do not pursue a re-evaluation to earn a right (101).

By choosing to accept we only amalgamate a privilege (99) and not a right (101), we are gifting an appreciation to another.

In gifting them our appreciation of their right (101) to posit their excellence standard definition, we are accepting a 99 and allowing them to exercise a 101.

This is love being gifted, gratitude in motion.

This allows us a win without the re-evaluation, as follows, as the second choice.

Our acceptance of the alternative, a 99 amalgamation, and resigning ourselves to accept the excellence standards of another validates as us recognizing another's excellence standard definition and provides for us, an interpretation allowance.

If we wish, to conquer our impatience to posit excellence standard definitions on the environment in which we subsist.

Our acceptance of this 99 is saying we are willing to accept others are in possession of rights (101) to posit their excellence standard definitions. And that their right and excellence standard definitions are greater.

Whether or not compared to us.

We are willing to accepting this position, not as a resignation of us being inferior but as a willingness to recognize the validity of the right (101) of another.

Ibn Ahmad

We are willing to gift love as a par inherently necessary in all endeavors to define excellence standard definitions.

# Chapter 14 - Eagerness

Eagerness here is the final challenge to us in conquering the 7s.

We are either in possession of the two 7s as a result of us successfully defending our right to posit excellence standard definitions on the environment in which we subsist up to the last chapter, or we are in possession of a single 7 for conquering impatience as a result of us accepting the acceptance put forward under the banner of love.

If we are in position of the two 7s as a result of a successful defense so far, our final challenge to defend them and amalgamate a 3$^{rd}$ 8 is eagerness.

In this instance, the threat of eagerness manifests in our desire to posit excellence standard definitions on the environment in which we subsist.

Although we have summated we possess a right, we must taper our espousal against the potential of it being interpreted as an imposition.

For if our espousal is to be interpreted as an imposition, we have lost at the very end and have not conquered impatience at all. We cannot have the total acceptance of our excellence standard definitions we targeted.

The foremost motivation for us to embark on an excellence standard definition act in the first place.

Hence, our espousal must guard against the threat of eagerness, even when we have an amalgamated right.

If we are in possession of a single 7 as a result of us accepting the validity of love as outlined in the previous chapter, we are conquering our own impatience which manifested in our desire to posit excellence standard definitions on our environment.

We are accepting another's posited excellence standard definitions, inherently conquering our impatience.

We no longer wish to define or posit our own excellence standard definitions.

The win here for the taking is to guard against our own eagerness to challenge the excellence standards definitions we accepted others possess a right to posit.

As we have accepted they possess a right to posit, we must find balance to accept their measurement.

To trust that they wish to get it right as much as you did.

After all, they have already earned the right to posit after applying the same standard of measurement as did you to earn a right in the first place.

The difference is, they amalgamated a right (101) while you amalgamate a privilege (99). The par setting standard used by you to determine rights must be trusted for use by another as you once trusted it for yourself.

If you can guard against the threat of eagerness, you will earn a 7 to conquer impatience and doubly by refusing to challenge, thereby conquering yourself.

So, either way, your own understanding of excellence standard definitions, their recognition and acceptance has allowed you to win the two 7s, and forge an amalgamation into a 3$^{rd}$ 8.

You are no longer impatient as you are willing to gift gratitude.

No floating dead wood praises with bags of insincerity.

We now understand and are ready for unions.

Marriages and Relationships.

The 3$^{rd}$ eight.

An amalgamation to morph Qad'r blockers.

Hues.

3rd 8 - Pie:

# Represent

# hues

# Chapter 15 - Life

**L** – License
**I** – Is
**F** – For
**E** – Effective hues

Allow passage.

# Chapter 16 - Trust

Trust a man when he is being tested.

# Chapter 17 - Patience

Patience is thankfulness.

# Chapter 18 - Thankfulness

Thankfulness is for hues reflection.

# Chapter 19 - Pleasure

Pleasure plus patience pleases.

# Chapter 20 - Greed

Greedy uses vase.

# Chapter 21 - Morph

Morph hues.

Say:

In the name of God,
The Beneficent, The Merciful.
Thaleeb-Khayah.

And blink repeatedly for ear passage clearance.

Good Day Brother – The lay away

By:

Ibn Ahmad
Sports & Spiritual Fitness and Wellness Guide

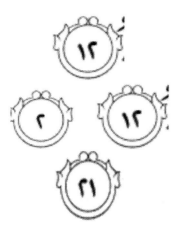

Tailoring acceptance

# Contents

- Rotate her ill

 - Tailor her aid

 - Give her take

 - Take her I will

# Introduction

The art of Aesthetics teaches responding and appreciating beauty.

Delivering your utmost attentive moment.

Not attentiveness measured through the measurement of time but one of a descriptive quotient.

Adorning with appreciation.

For example the smile an object of beauty elucidates in us.

The way our attention magnetizes us to it.

A captivating silence that expresses our will to seek new words of expression.

Appreciating the way we are inspired with moments of laugh-out-loud jolts.

Laughter.

Our finding of congruency with another.

That form of adornment.

Giving back what is a fair elucidation in us.

What is brought out in us.

Why is it valuable for our attention?

Why do we find it unites us?

Why does it elucidate in us a fairness of expression we find undeniable?

Why does our smile tells of our interpretation?

Of its' beauty?

Of its' kinks?

Of its' story?

Our giggles may say of failed attempts we interpret.

Why does it make us appreciate?

Express?

Adorn?

Is it a choice and not an imperative of the honest kind?

Why?

Because it brings alive in us our beauty recognition faculty. Our God faculty.

We learn to appreciate.

To value smiles.

Why our thoughts should be of the positive kind.

How does an object of beauty do this?

Is it because of the presence of beautification ingredients?

And if so, what are these beautification ingredients.

In this book, we posit it is one ingredient.

Aesthetics.

The art of adornment.

The location of beauty in whatever our eyes set themselves on.

In this book, we further posit that a beauty creation process is inherent in every created thing.

Even the creation of beauty.

And to enhance our awareness of appreciative beauty, we must first find elucidation of the beauty creation process.

As wherever beauty is found, a creative process was involved, our recognition must recognize through an intuitive process.

In this book, we propose a 12 step journey of beauty creation hoping it will make fortuitous our beauty recognition faculty.

Elucidating acceptance as the one step in the beauty creation process in aid of our education.

The journey we propose in the 12 steps is one of recognition, melting and blending and rewarding.

The twelve 21 postulation change is a happiness flip that progresses a 1 to 2 to a 2 to 1 change.

The rationale this promotes is as follows. A movement of 1 to 2 represents a move to division while a movement from 2 to 1 represents unification.

Division unified.

# Methodology

Nothingness is hubris.

The Merriam-Webster online version provides the following definition for the word hubris:

"great pride...", (extract.)

The 12 step methodology this book follows is applied the following way, to deliver a way.

The way to the Happiness line is the tailoring of an acceptance.

The first step, Step 1 identifies an individual act of selflessness. An act of identification.

An honest recognition.

**Process    -    1**

Steps 2 to 8 follows a melt and blend process. Accentuating and accumulating.

Stone setting.

**Process    -    2**

Steps 9 to 12 is reward recognition.

## Process          -          3

The opening statement, hubris is nothingness, earns its right of inclusion as follows.

In the creation of anything, the relevant value delivered to the eyes of the creator in his endeavors of value creation for adornment is not non-control of his cost.

His etiquette is his measure of cost control.

In the first process, his honesty is tested.

In the next process, his patience is.

In the final process, his acceptance is.

If he wishes to deliver happiness and prove his theory of beauty creation, he must:

-          sacrifice first;

-          work second;

-          lead with acceptance third.

In the first two processes, the creator's great pride must be immeasurable.

In the third Process, his theory for creating a thing of beauty for another to appreciate is firstly dependent on his ability to locate the beauty value.

We must firstly adorn to find beauty.

And it is our tailoring of an acceptance of the outcome, in which the happiness switch is delivered.

The aesthetical process is successful only if beauty is recognized, enjoyed and transferred.

If the creator is able to do this, we will discover the happiness line the process targeted.

Discovery of the line is proven if there is a distributable reward and Process 3 provides the evidence. They are:

- the original item of value used in Process 1;

and

- the duplicate created by the process for distribution.

We can only perform an act that is beneficially in aid of another if we can prove the act is firstly of beneficial to us.

The returning of the item loaned to the process proves this.

Plus 1.

On evidence of this, our value creation process has earned its beatification veil.

Beauty's hallmark.

# Twelve 21 – The Acceptance

In each of the 12 chapters of this book, we propose a potential flip scenario.

Scenarios one can hopefully use to turn their doldrums to happiness.

The numbers twelve 21 attempt to prove where the flip exists.

As each of the scenarios in the 12 chapters offers a flip, it is up to the user to retire his hubris count and choose an act befitting the scenario value creation method.

The act he chooses to provide beneficial value to him and to others inherently contains the flip line.

The number of scenarios presented serves the purpose acceptance:

The key is here energy.

The value creation process we are proposing is the value of our energy finding enhancement.

Step 21.

The step of adornment.

It is our selection of an acceptance of the existence of a happiness enhancement that creates energy.

We believe when we can see.

We find when we can be.

If we believe when we can bear.

We beautify when we can contribute.

It is not a mathematical equation.

It is the light switch we will discover in our search.

To find contentment.

Accept this.

Rise with sunshine at 6. Here, there or everywhere, the sun rises.